PATIENCE STRONG'S
BIRTHDAY BOOK

PATIENCE STRONG'S

BIRTHDAY BOOK

Daily readings in prose and verse

Frederick Muller

First published in Great Britain 1955
by Frederick Muller Ltd., Fleet Street, London, E.C.4

Copyright © 1955, Patience Strong
This large-type edition first published 1971
Standard edition reprinted 1957, 1959, 1961, 1967

Reproduced and Printed in Great Britain by
Redwood Press Limited, Trowbridge & London
Bound by Wm. Brendon & Son Ltd., Tiptree
SBN: 584 10622 X (large-type edition)
SBN: 584 10748 X (standard edition)

TO MY FATHER

He taught me the things that every child should know,
Things about gardens — how to plant and sow.
A love of walking, striding stick in hand
Down the green ways of Nature's wonderland.

January 1st

MAY the way that lies ahead be lit with sunny gleams—and prove to be the road to the fulfilment of your dreams. May it lead you to the place where lost hopes are restored—Where love is true and life is good and faith has its reward.

o o o o o o

January 2nd

BIRTHDAYS are the gateways of the future,
    May this one,
Open into pleasant places
    Out into the sun.
Showing you the pathway of Tomorrow bright
    and clear.
God be with you at the gateway of another year.

o o o o o o

January 3rd

DO not let the unknown future fill you with dismay. It is in the hands of God, so go upon your way. Trust in Him and have no fear. You do not walk alone. He leads the faithful in the dark and careth for His own.

January 4th

RAISE the edifice of life upon foundations strong and sure. Put the best into your task and build with things that will endure. With the tools of hope and patience fashion something true and fine. Scorning all that would destroy the harmony of your design.

January 5th

OPEN the windows of my mind that I may catch the morning light. Grant me, Lord, a wide horizon, and a vision broad and bright. Give me eyes to seek for beauty and a heart to understand. Ears to hear the voice of conscience, feet to run at Love's command.

January 6th

ONE year older ; one year wiser may you prove to be. One year nearer to the thing you've worked for faithfully .... Count each a friend who comes with gifts for hand and heart—a friend who leaves you happier when it is time to part.

January 7th

THE world was never meant to be an earthly paradise. We are here to learn the way of love and sacrifice. Here to do the Master's bidding, servants of His will. With a duty to perform, a purpose to fulfil.

o o o o o o

January 8th

GOD'S unfailing goodness is a current deep and strong. Trust it and you'll find that it will carry you along. Take the risk and fling yourself on His omnipotence. Leave the shallows. Get into the stream of Providence.

o o o o o o

January 9th

MAKE an adventure of all that you do,
    Do it with humour and zest,
Looking at life from the broad point of view,
Giving your utmost and best.

January 10*th*

THIS is an imperfect world as you will surely find — and if you would be happy in it you must bear in mind — that things are as they are. Life can't go always as you plan. You have to work with broken tools and do the best you can.

    o   *o*   *o*   *o*   *o*   *o*

January 11*th*

DO not count the years but count the blessings they've bestowed.
And the many friends that you have made along the road.
Do not count the birthdays, let them come and let them go.
Time is not your enemy unless you make it so.

    o   *o*   *o*   *o*   *o*   *o*

January 12*th*

BELIEVE in the future though dark be the sky. The storm will pass over. The clouds will roll by. Believe in the best though it's hidden from view. For this is the faith that will carry you through.

January 13*th*

W E are given strength to bear the burdens of
      each day,
Grace sufficient for the hour and light to see the
    way.
Whether in the vale of shadows or on heights
    sublime,
Live your life with hope and courage. One day
    at a time.

January 14*th*

S O long as you can pray when all your world
      has gone awry,
So long as you can sing when there are rain clouds
    in the sky.
So long as you can cling to hope when luck has
    passed you by,
    You will come out smiling in the end.

January 15*th*

L IFE should be a festival of hope and merri-
    ment — with everyone in high and happy
mood. Every day that passes should be well and
truly spent — and hearts be lifted up in gratitude.

January 16th

TACKLE something truly great and aim at something high. You don't know what you can achieve until you really try. Do not be content to take life's joys and pull no weight. Man was made for enterprises glorious and great.

January 17th

LIFE is what you make it, bright or gloomy it can be. Your mental outlook colours everything you do and see. Your world may wear a dingy air or have a rosy glow. It all depends on what you think, for " thinking makes it so."

January 18th

THIS may be the very day that you've been praying for,
The day on which Good Luck will come aknocking at your door.
Bringing you that long awaited opportunity,
So greet it in a happy mood of gay expectancy.

January 19th

WISHES will not lead you to the things you
would possess.
Wishes will not bring to you the prizes of success.
But work and faith will surely get you where you
want to be.
Effort and determination spell prosperity.

⌀   ⌀   ⌀   ⌀   ⌀   ⌀

January 20th

MAKE a resolution as your birthday dawns
once more — To be a nicer sort of person
than you were before.   To be a little wiser and
improve upon the past.   And make the coming
year a little better than the last.

⌀   ⌀   ⌀   ⌀   ⌀   ⌀

January 21st

DO not choose the easy task or seek the safest
road.   Do not shirk the sharing and the
bearing of the load.   Obstacles you will encounter
on the way ahead — but do not shrink from difficulties . . . . Conquer them instead.

January 22nd

WE do not always get the thing we aimed for at the start. The sweet desire of early youth, the dear wish of the heart. But through our disappointments God's own wisdom we can trace. Something is denied — but something better takes its place.

o   o   o   o   o   o

January 23rd

THE best and sweetest things in life are things you cannot buy : the music of the birds at dawn, the rainbow in the sky. The dazzling magic of the stars, the miracle of light. The precious gifts of health and strength, of hearing, speech and sight.

o   o   o   o   o   o

January 24th

WHILE you're waiting for the future, don't forget to keep in view — all the good and all the joy that life today can offer you. Go on dreaming of the harvest and of what the year may bring — But make the winter yield a blessing while you're waiting for the Spring.

January 25th

I T'S the light of happiness when shining in the mind — that makes the day look bright to you and life seem good and kind. It's the inner sunshine gives your world a smiling face — and helps you see the loveliness behind the commonplace.

January 26th

D O not be discouraged if you don't seem to advance.
Do not be downhearted in the face of circumstance.
It is not the speed that matters as the road you trace.
Be content to jog on at a good and steady pace.

January 27th

W E can't undo what has been done and what was said we can't unsay. We can't go back and live again a single hour of yesterday. We have to take life as it is and learn to face the present scene — never wasting time and thought upon the things that might have been.

January 28th

WHEN you feel that your courage is sagging—
It's not easy to work up a smile. There are rough bits of road on all journeys, for it couldn't be smooth all the while. But when tempted to think of misfortunes — think too of how much you've been blessed. Don't brood on the worst life has brought you, and fail to remember the best.

o   o   o   o   o   o

January 29th

THROUGH the stark limbs of the trees no sap is rising yet — But soon upon the leafless boughs the blossom will be set. In a way most marvellous that no man can explain. There will be a resurrection. Spring will come again.

o   o   o   o   o   o

January 30th

THERE'S time for all you have to do,
And time to dream a little too,
But none to spare for sighs and tears
Wishing back the bygone years.

January 31st

IF you do not try to force the pace of Providence,
    Time will work things out and with a happy
        consequence.
Difficult your life may be and hard your present
    plight,
But wait before you grumble.   Give Time time to
    put it right.

                                                 ⌀   ⌀   ⌀   ⌀   ⌀   ⌀

February 1st

WE cannot halt the pace of Time, the clocks
    go ticking on. When birthdays come
along we say " Another year has gone."   But let
it go without regret whatever it has brought.
Greet the future with a happy and courageous
thought—welcoming another year, believing hopefully—that the worst's behind you and " the best
is yet to be."

February 2nd

DON'T expect a heaven in a world like this.
    Don't look for perfection or for flawless
        bliss.
Take life as you find it with its joy and pain
Bearing with good humour YOUR part of the
    strain.

B

February 3rd

BLESSINGS seem to fall upon the joyous and
    the gay.
Fortune is attracted by a smile.
Lady Luck will join you if you go the sunny way
And will walk beside you all the while.

                  o   o   o   o   o   o

February 4th

REMEMBER that the darkness often veils a
    mystery—and conceals the shape of all the
good that is to be . . . . Just keep going bravely on
and confident remain—until God rolls the shadow
back and sends the sun again.

                  o   o   o   o   o   o

February 5th

GREET your birthday morning with a bright
    and smiling face. Turn your little world
into a good and happy place. Ask a blessing.
Pray that you'll be strengthened, helped and led.
Take a new self out upon the road that lies ahead.

February 6th

WE do not always reap in every field—the sort of crop we hoped that it would yield. But often we have found in time of need—we've gathered where we've never sown a seed.

February 7th

PROFIT by everything. Wrest good from ill. Double your assets of wisdom and skill. Increase your happiness. Add to your friends. Turn to advantage whatever Fate sends.

February 8th

IT'S your thoughts that matter. What you think within your heart—will decide if you're to play a mean or noble part. Lift your thoughts on wings of prayer. There is no better way—of beginning and of ending every passing day.

February 9th

WITHIN yourself you have the power to be what you desire. To reach the shining goal to which your hopes and dreams aspire. Not in realms of fantasy, but in your heart and mind—The magic you'll discover and the secret you will find.

                         ⚬   ⚬   ⚬   ⚬   ⚬   ⚬

February 10th

LOOKING back, we see it was the hardship not the ease—that taught us most of life's philosophy. The hurt in things, the stabs and stings that brought us to our knees—To learn new wisdom from calamity.

                         ⚬   ⚬   ⚬   ⚬   ⚬   ⚬

February 11th

WE have had to go a-seeking for the treasures we have bought—But our friends, the best and dearest, these have come to us unsought. Life has crossed our paths with theirs when quite by chance we've turned a bend—and God has led us to the place where we have made another friend.

February 12th

THE whole world's woes you cannot bear.
But you can halve your neighbour's share,
And on the path that now you tread,
A little sunshine you can shed.

February 13th

YOU must have a plan and a purpose. Though
swiftly the years may depart—You'll always
have something to live for—if you have a dream
in your heart.

February 14th

LOOK at life with eyes that see the best things,
not the bad. Cherish in your memory the
good times, not the sad. Choose the bright side
of the road where sunshine lights the way. Walk
in the direction of the blue sky, not the grey.

February 15th

LET Hope be your companion along life's
winding road. When the skies are stormy
and heavy is the load—She will point you on-
wards to that distant star. Keep Hope close
beside you and you'll travel far.

February 16*th*

THE happy heart is that which is content with little things. The heart that loves a simple life, the heart in which there springs—a sense of joy with each fresh day, a prayer of gratitude—for the morning miracle of health and strength renewed.

February 17*th*

TRUST in God a little more and let Him work things out. When around your path the shadows fall. " Be not anxious for the morrow." Never fear or doubt. It may never happen after all.

February 18*th*

GLADLY let us face the future knowing all is well—thankful for the good things we've received, for who can tell ? Though with golden happiness the past years have been blessed—The years that lie ahead may be the brightest and the best.

February 19th

GAY be your heart and happy be the hours,
    Whether you walk in sunshine or in
        showers.
Bright be your life with friendships fond and true.
Blessings be yours and Time be kind to you.

February 20th

WE think we know what's best for us. We
    plan and plot and scheme—to reach the
shining goal we have in view. But oftentimes
we find we have to dream another dream—and
build another castle in the blue.

February 21st

ONE by one Time steals away the good and
    golden years—leaving us our recollections
and our souvenirs . . . . so that when the winter
comes wherever we may be—we can always pluck
the wayside flowers of memory.

February 22nd

DO not let the flight of Time depress you or alarm. Don't resist the passing years. Grow old with grace and charm. Keep the simple faith of childhood if you would possess— the secret joy which is the source of all true happiness.

❧ ❧ ❧ ❧ ❧ ❧

February 23rd

SOMEONE'S got to stitch the golden threads into the grey. Someone's got to make the music on a dreary day. Someone's got to clear the clouds and let the sunlight through. Some- one's got to brighten up the world. So why not you ?

❧ ❧ ❧ ❧ ❧ ❧

February 24th

DO not be discouraged if the trail is taking you—Far away from all the shining goals you had in view . . . . Fate has something else in store. Press on and you will see. There are many turnings on the road of destiny.

February 25th

WHEN a birthday comes along you turn a clean white page — Another chapter to commence, whatever be your age. Although the story of the past was one of want and woe. This can be a new beginning if you will it so.

           o o o o o o

February 26th

OUR minds like houses shabby grow.
    A sudden flash of truth will show
How much we need to sweep away
The dusty thoughts of yesterday.

           o o o o o o

February 27th

IF you never lose your sense of joy and gratitude.
    Day by day within your spirit youth will be renewed. If in " every common bush " God's glory you behold. Let the years roll by ! You'll be a long time growing old.

February 28th

SEASONS pass in Love's green garden and the years their changes bring. But beneath the fallen blossoms hope takes root and new joys spring. Round the arbours of remembrance, flowers of friendship ever climb—and the mosses of affection grow between the stones of Time.

March 1st

BIRTHDAYS seem to bring to mind our childhood memories—and to wake an echo of forgotten melodies. Happy birthdays of the past ! The heart recalls once more—the parties and the presents and the postman at the door. Happy birthdays of the future ! Many may there be—bringing blessings of contentment and felicity.

March 2nd

DWELL not on the things that fill the heart with sad regret. The past has gone, so let it go. Your grievances forget. Remember only this, that Fortune follows in the train—of those who have the pluck and courage to begin again.

March 3rd

OPEN the windows of faith today and pray that a wind will blow your way — To scatter all thoughts of doubt and fear—and bring you a message of hope and cheer.

March 4th

TIME brings many changes, turning golden hairs to grey. But if the heart is young we grow not old. It's always May. The young in heart look through the clouds and see the golden gleam—because they never lose the power to laugh, to hope, to dream.

March 5th

WE need no other rosary if we can string our days with beads — of friendliness and charity, of loving thoughts and kindly deeds. For everything we do or say to ease the strain and calm the strife — adds another bead of beauty to the rosary of life.

March 6th

IF your mood is gloomy — break it. If you want the sunshine — make it. Though the sky be leaden and the thunder loud. Go you singing through the storm. It will turn out fair and warm — If you sew a silver lining in the cloud.

March 7th

WELCOME the new. Let go the old. Mourn not the things now ended. Have you not dreamed a brave new dream and seen the vision splendid ? Great is the goodness of the Lord. Go forth and have no fear — Out into the golden promise of another year.

March 8th

THINK not of the hopes that failed, but of the wishes that came true. The answered prayer, the dream fulfilled, the cloudy sky that turned to blue. Brood not on the disappointments, but remember on this day : how God's love has been around you all the while and all the way.

March 9th

WE were meant to share the lovely things that heaven sends. Joys are doubled, sorrows halved, when we are with our friends . . . . And fortunate are they who looking back with smiles and tears — can trace the thread of Friendship through the pattern of the years.

March 10th

FRIEND of my soul, leave me not, I pray Thee,
Lost and alone on life's winding way.
In Thy dear Presence I fear no evil,
Walk Thou beside me night and day.

March 11th

FATE is fickle like the vane that turns upon the spire. The winds don't always blow just in the quarter you desire. Learn to take with cheerfulness whatever comes your way — for life is like the weather, sometimes sunny, sometimes grey.

March 12*th*

FIND your joy in simple things, for money cannot buy — the music of a blackbird or the rainbow in the sky — the fragrance of the roses and the stars at eventide. All the green and golden glory of the countryside.

            ◦   ◦   ◦   ◦   ◦   ◦

March 13*th*

WE are on a journey and we are not here to stay. That is why we have to make the most of every day. We plot and scheme and plan and dream and build our castles high — But often we forget that we are only passing by.

            ◦   ◦   ◦   ◦   ◦   ◦

March 14*th*

NEVER let your trials and troubles fill you with dismay. There's a purpose in them all as you will find one day. Often the calamities are blessings in disguise. The things that make us humble are the things that make us wise.

March 15th

IN life there is no going back. The road lies straight ahead. You can't return along the track to seek out what is dead . . . . Your past mistakes you can't undo and wishing is in vain. But don't forget it's true that you can always try again.

o   o   o   o   o   o

March 16th

THERE are windows in the mind and we should keep them clean—so that when we're looking out upon life's changing scene—we see a vision beautiful, a landscape fair and bright— Glorified at every point by the eternal Light.

o   o   o   o   o   o

March 17th

HAPPINESS is never found by searching here and there. You've got to take it with you where you go. If you've got it in your heart you'll find it everywhere — and everything will wear a rosy glow.

March 18*th*

MAKE a vow to live for NOW and not the unknown morrow. Make the most of present joys expecting more to follow. Your future lies in God's own hands. Be thankful it is so. Surely there is nothing more you need to ask or know.

o   o   o   o   o   o

March 19*th*

DO not look for easy paths, but see your shoes are strong—so that when the track is stony you can get along. Don't go shod for pleasant ways but for the uphill climb—then you'll be prepared for any road at any time.

o   o   o   o   o   o

March 20*th*

YOU will never grow old if you have a goal and a purpose to achieve. You will never grow old if you have the power to hope and to believe. You will always be young if you take your place in the march of new ideas—for you'll have the zest and the best of youth . . . . with the wisdom of the years.

March 21st

IT is a lovely and wonderful thing — to be born on the very first day of the Spring. To enter the world as the Winter grows old — and the daffodils open their trumpets of gold.

o o o o o o

March 22nd

LIFE is double-sided ; there's a wrong side and a right. A sad side and a happy side, a black side and a bright. So if things seem dark to you just change your thoughts about. Life will look quite different if you turn it best side out.

o o o o o o

March 23rd

TIME is precious. Do not waste it. Use it carefully. Think before you fritter it away. Time is Life : your little portion of eternity— the part that lies before you now, today.

o o o o o o

March 24th

WE all have a share of the woes and the blows. At least, you can't say Life is tame. The building, the breaking—the giving, the taking . . . . It's all a part of the game.

c

March 25th

WHO would want an easy creed ?
      Heaven would be cheap indeed,
If we did not pay with tears
For the wisdom of the years.

⋄ ⋄ ⋄ ⋄ ⋄ ⋄

March 26th

WHEN the evening shadows fall — May the quiet heart recall — not the troubles of the day, but small mercies by the way : the unexpected gift bestowed — the friend you met along the road. Not the things you failed to do — but the wishes that came true.

⋄ ⋄ ⋄ ⋄ ⋄ ⋄

March 27th

IF the root is deep enough the tree of life will grow — lovelier as the years advance, although the storms may blow — and shake the blossoms from the boughs in gusts of wind and rain. God always sends another Spring. The sap will rise again.

March 28th

LORD, give me light upon my way — and wisdom for each passing day — that I may prove what I profess — continuing in faithfulness.

       o   o   o   o   o   o

March 29th

DREAM a little, not too much. Just enough to give a touch — of splendour to the darkest day : a bright edge to the cloud of grey. Enough to keep within your heart — as one by one the years depart — the magic of the golden days : the power to see with youth's clear gaze.

       o   o   o   o   o   o

March 30th

FOLLOW your star, the star of fate that leads you know not where. Follow the secret trail of faith, made bold by hope and prayer. Follow the music of your dreams beyond the last ascent. Fear not the hazards of the way for God is provident.

March 31st

HOUR by hour and day by day fresh beauties burst upon our sight. The trees once dark against the sky are caught in webs of golden light. Outlines soften, colours deepen. New songs echo down the lane. A miracle is happening. The world is being born again.

o   o   o   o   o   o

April 1st

THOUGH the years take much away and Time be rapid in its flight — I pray I never fail to find my joy, my peace and my delight — in Nature's sweet companionship, the music of the mountain rills — the fragrant lanes, the furrowed fields, the deep green woods, the windy hills.

o   o   o   o   o   o

April 2nd

SEEN from the shadows through windows shut fast — the future is veiled in the mists of the past. But eyes that can see with a faith big and bold — look through the clouds to horizons of gold.

April 3rd

GIVE me ears to hear Thy voice in every human plea, and through all discords to discern potential harmony. Give me thoughts that bear me up when life would crush me low. Give me eyes to see Thy light wherever I may go.

April 4th

BENEFITS and boons and blessings, mercies big and small. Add them up. You'll find life's not so hopeless after all. Difficulties may increase and cares be multiplied — but don't forget to count the entries on the credit side.

April 5th

YOU are not the only pilgrim on this bit of road. Everyone must pass this way and each must bear his load. But faith shall justify itself and lost things be restored — the weary heart be comforted and love have its reward.

April 6th

EVERY dawn is a miracle. We wake to life once more. Every morn is a key that opens yet another door. Every day is a precious gift that God bestows on you — and an opportunity to prove yourself anew.

o   o   o   o   o   o

April 7th

EVERY passing phase of life brings something to remember. April dreams, and Junetide joys to brighten grey December. Every changing season brings its own sweet consolations. Time may fade the flowers, but there are always compensations.

o   o   o   o   o   o

April 8th

MAY you find contentment and tranquillity of mind. May Time's finger touch you lightly and the years be kind. Blessings round your path unfold and happiness increase. God be gracious, granting you prosperity and peace.

April 9th

TAKE the compass of your faith and brave the far unknown. Dare to strike out on the deep adventuring alone. Don't stand waiting on the quay, just weaving idle schemes. Take a boat and row right out to meet your ship of dreams.

∘ ∘ ∘ ∘ ∘ ∘

April 10th

WHEN you know that round the bend decisions must be made. Pray for guidance. Keep right on and do not be afraid . . . . You won't take the wrong direction or be led astray, if you read the signposts that God sets along the way.

∘ ∘ ∘ ∘ ∘ ∘

April 11th

DOES it really matter when the first grey hair appears ? No-one's getting younger and we can't hold back the years. Time goes on regardless of our efforts and our tears. We're only here a lifetime after all.

April 12*th*

IT'S fatal to procrastinate and then to put the blame on Fate — because you find it's just too late . . . . Tomorrow never comes.

o   o   o   o   o   o

April 13*th*

IF you see the funny side you'll always walk the sunny side and come out smiling through the stress and strife. So cultivate the power to see— the little touch of comedy behind the trials and tragedies of life.

o   o   o   o   o   o

April 14*th*

LIFE upon this little globe is just an episode. A journey : and we pass but once along this bit of road. So do to others as you would that they should do to you. You will not come this way again. You're only passing through.

o   o   o   o   o   o

April 15*th*

IF when you wake you can take the bright view. You'll always look out on a world fresh and new — And life will hold endless surprises for you — because you will never grow old.

April 16*th*

SCATTER seeds of friendship, thoughts and words and deeds. Though the soil looks stony, scatter wide your seeds. Every kindly action, every word sincere — every good intention meant to help or cheer, is a seed of friendship and somewhere, someday — it will root and blossom in its own sweet way.

April 17*th*

FAITH removes mountains. Faith heals. Faith restores. Faith scoffs at logic, rough paths and locked doors. Faith laughs at obstacles. Faith goes right on — when the last word's been said and the last hope has gone.

April 18*th*

THE riddle of existence is beyond us. Let's admit — that though we're clever we don't really know the half of it. But we know there is a Power behind the mystery. A Mind that knows the answer and a God who holds the key.

April 19*th*

THE love that runs with eager feet to do the thankless tasks — The love that seeks for no reward, the sort of love that asks — the chance to do a little more, but never any less. This is the kind of love that brings the greatest happiness.

o o o o o o

April 20*th*

WAIT before you worry. It will all come right. Why be in a hurry, Trouble to invite. Don't get in a flurry, giving way to doubt. Pray before you worry. Let Time work things out.

o o o o o o

April 21*st*

LOOK forward with a hopeful mind. Look forward !
Resolve to leave the past behind. Look forward !
You can't afford to let your gaze
Turn back to rest on other days,
Down brighter better broader ways — Look forward.

April 22nd

ONE life and one alone you have to live upon
this little earth.   One life in which to learn
so much, to seek and find and prove your worth.
The gold of Time is yours to squander — or with
care to use and spend.   Waste it not in fruitless
quests that get you nowhere in the end.

April 23rd

O HAPPY day that brings to mind the little
Stratford Street — where England's greatest
bard was born and countless pilgrims meet — To
walk the banks of Avon and to feed the sacred
flame — that burns around the memory of that
immortal name.

April 24th

SHINE and shower ! They come together all
along the way. Life with all its ups and
downs is like an April day.   It's easy to go smiling
through the bright and sunny hours — but we
have to learn to go a-singing through the showers.

April 25th

BE true to the best that is in you. Be upright and fair and sincere. Stoop not to the smallest deception. Have nothing to hide or to fear. And when the last task is completed — the last battle over and won — the voice of the Master will greet you with " Well done, good servant, well done."

April 26th

WHAT are ends but new beginnings ? Journeys end and friends depart . . . . But there is always another chapter in the story of the heart.

April 27th

O MAY the first prayer of my day be always one of thankfulness. Thankful may I always be if Fate sends failure or success. Thankful for the blows and blessings and the mercies shown to me. Thankful for the undertones as well as for the melody.

April 28th

STRANGE is life's music. Some is gay and some in minor key. But sad and sweetest tones must blend to make the harmony. That's what makes the song of life into a symphony : mingled notes of rapture, sorrow and felicity.

April 29th

ONE kind thought can work great wonders. One small rift can break a cloud. One brave heart can strengthen many. One bright word can cheer a crowd. One good soul can give to others something that will be a stay— when they're toiling up the hill and there are shadows round the way.

April 30th

A COVENANT of mercy the Lord has made with man — and when across the heavens we see a rainbow's span — We know that God is making His promises anew. We know the pledge is certain. We know His word is true.

May 1*st*

THE new-born lamb, the fledgling bird, the buttercup, the honey bee. The pregnant earth, the greening wheat, the flush of bloom on bush and tree. Once again the flowers are blowing and the songbirds call their mates. Spring returns in all its glory. Man destroys and God creates.

May 2*nd*

YOU can't retrace your steps in life. The road goes winding on. You can't return along the track in search of what has gone. You have to keep right on and use the light that's given you — your own small mission to fulfil, your purpose to pursue.

May 3*rd*

EVEN in the midst of crowds the heart in silent prayer — can hold a brief communion for God is always there. A moment in His presence is enough to heal and bless — and carry you through many hours of work and weariness.

May 4th

IF you travel your road with a faith in your
heart, it will give you the courage to grope—
up through the valleys of failure and fear, spurred
by a wonderful hope. While you have faith you
will feel every day the urge to go forth with a
smile—believing you'll find when you've climbed
the last hill, the Something that makes all worth
while.

⸰ ⸰ ⸰ ⸰ ⸰ ⸰

May 5th

BUILD your castles, but remember dreams are
not enough. Castles must be underpinned
with sterner stronger stuff. Courage and determination, faith and energy — You will need to
turn your dream into reality.

⸰ ⸰ ⸰ ⸰ ⸰ ⸰

May 6th

IF you have the power to take the bright and
rosy view. It will bring you smiling through
the worst that Fate can do. None can take it
from you if this treasure you possess — for it is
the gift of God : the gift of happiness.

May 7th

THERE'S no meaning in the creed that I repeat each day — unless I try to live it as I go upon my way. There's no meaning in the words unless they strengthen me — and give me faith to face the challenge of adversity.

May 8th

LET us be content, my soul, with what the years have brought. We desired a heaven, but it seems that we were caught—in the net of mundane things. Life did not bring romance. We trod the old prosaic path of humdrum circumstance. And yet it has been good, my soul, for looking back today—I see there was a golden light on the familiar way.

May 9th

WALLFLOWERS in the cottage gardens. Hawthorn in the lane. Bluebells in the dappled woods and buttercups again. Apple-blossom in the orchards. Swallows on the wing. Could Heaven be more beautiful than England in the Spring ?

May 10*th*

THERE'S a special job in life that you were meant to do. That is why you're where you are. God set that task for you. Not along some other road, but where your ways now lie — is the place that you and you alone can occupy.

◦ ◦ ◦ ◦ ◦ ◦

May 11*th*

WHEN you look back over the way you've come and start to count the miles — you often find that half the fun was getting over the stiles .... It wasn't the smooth and easy bit that brought the greatest thrill. It was clambering over the obstacles and pushing up the hill.

◦ ◦ ◦ ◦ ◦ ◦

May 12*th*

GIVE Fear no lodging in your house, no place in which to dwell. Bar him out of every thought and know that all is well. God giveth strength sufficient for each day and its demands. Trust and fear not for the morrow. Leave it in His hands.

D

May 13*th*

THERE are ruts in the road on life's stony street. There are dangerous places for stumbling feet, where the strongest have fallen and cowards turned back — to look for a safer and easier track. But remember that under Time's rutted clay — the steps of the Master have marked the way.

May 14*th*

KEEP the lamp of friendship burning with a sure and steady glow. Feed it with the oil of kindness. Never let the flame get low. Old friends, new friends, welcome them within the warm room of your heart — then lonely you will never be as one by one the years depart.

May 15*th*

WHEN the day is over may I know within my heart — that I've tried to do my duty and have played my part. Given all I had to give and followed faithfully — on the path where I believed Thy hand was leading me.

May 16*th*

THE world is full of clocks that tick our litt｜ ﹅ lives away. We cannot halt or hold ﾟ ｌe minutes of the passing day. So make the m｀st of every one, the sunshine and the showers — a｀d fill your heart with memories of good and hap｀ y hours.

o   o   o   o   o   o

May 17*th*

THE heart is a house of many rooms where things are stored away : the treasures of life's remembered joys, the pearls of yesterday . . . . But there is a corner of the heart, a secret place where we — Cherish above all other things . . . . a Mother's memory.

o   o   o   o   o   o

May 18*th*

TOMORROW ! . . . . Would you really wish to see into that unknown land ? Sufficient for the heart to know that everything is in God's hand. It's only in the present moment that your life is yours to live. So take with joy and thankfulness the utmost that it has to give.

May 19*th*

HERE and there upon life's path a broken stone appears. Yet Time is kind — and in the crazy paving of the years — it covers up the jagged cracks and hides them from our sight — with the moss of sweet remembrance ever green and bright.

o o o o o o

May 20*th*

EVERY phase of life should teach,
      Something new. And so we reach
The point at which the heart can rest
Knowing all is for the best.

o o o o o o

May 21*st*

JUST keep going — knowing that you'll get there in the end — Just keep showing you believe there's something round the bend . . . . Many falter when misfortune's icy winds come blowing — but those who live to reach their goals are those who just keep going.

May 22nd

SEE all the beauty the world has to show.   Take all the blessings that Life can bestow.   Hear all the music and pluck all the flowers — making the most of the wonderful hours.   Quickly, too quickly, the years slip away.   Walk while you can in the sunshine of May.

May 23rd

STRENGTH for the day.   That is all that I ask. Light for my guidance and zest for my task. Peace and contentment, a quiet abode And grace for my soul at the end of the road.

May 24th

IF we could plan our lives there'd be no trials, no tears, no loss.   But then how should we ever learn the meaning of the Cross ?   If all went well we'd never need to kneel and close our eyes— and never learn about the things that make us strong and wise.

May 25th

TIDES of Time roll in and bring — Summer, Autumn, Winter, Spring. Tides of Life . . . . they ebb and flow — leaving driftwood as they go. Search the shore and you will find — what the tide has left behind.

∘ ∘ ∘ ∘ ∘ ∘

May 26th

BLOSSOMTIDE in England, cherry, plum and pear. Flowering apple orchards . . . . What could be more fair ? Yet the bloom must wither and the beauty go. The blossoms must be scattered that the fruit might grow. Nature's ways are perfect. She must work her will. Springtime gives the promise Summer days fulfil.

∘ ∘ ∘ ∘ ∘ ∘

May 27th

HAVE your schemes all fallen through ? Have you got to start anew ? Maybe it is good or you. Why worry ? . . . . Do your best and do your share. Keep straight on and don't despair. If you've said your daily prayer — Why worry ?

May 28*th*

GIVE me patience for the humdrum duties. Keep me humble, never seeking praise. Make me conscious of the things of beauty — as I go about my quiet ways . . . . Make me wise for there are problems pressing. Make me calm amidst the storm and strife. Make me worthy to receive Thy blessing — glad and grateful for the boon of life.

May 29*th*

YOU have two hands, so take with one and with the other give. That's the way that life works out and that's the way to live. What you get and what you give must balance up some-day. It's give a little, take a little, all along the way.

May 30*th*

LEAVE the world a little better for your tiny span. The good you do may go unnoticed by your fellow man — but it is recorded, every detail, every phase. An unseen pen is writing out the story of your days.

May 31*st*

GO through the day with a song in your heart.
Doing your duty and playing your part.
Harness the hours so that none is ill spent—
wherever you are being glad and content . . . .
Keep a wise check on the unruly tongue—ready
to learn from the old and the young.   Taking what
comes with a smile and a jest—facing life squarely
and giving your best.

June 1*st*

THIS is what we dream about all through the
winter gloom.   The good and golden season
when the roses are in bloom.   When ramblers
cover fence and wall and bushes in the bed—
glow in lovely tones of yellow, white and pink
and red.

June 2*nd*

THOUGH the wise console us with philosophies
profound — no man knows from whence we
come and whither we are bound.   All we know
is this : that we are pilgrims passing by.   So
why waste time in asking questions . . . . Where
and how and why.

June 3rd

LOOK at life through sunlit windows and you'll always see — something lovely, something good wherever you may be. Clear away the dust of fear and let no smear remain. Look at every problem through a sunny windowpane.

◦ ◦ ◦ ◦ ◦ ◦

June 4th

IN the garden of your life may Junetide joys remain. Roses never wither and the summer never wane. And should the winter ever come and bring the cold winds blowing — May you never fail to find the flowers of friendship growing.

◦ ◦ ◦ ◦ ◦ ◦

June 5th

SAINTS and sages tell us what to do and how to live. Many clever books are written. Good advice they give. But the secret in one little phrase can be enshrined . . . . Just be kind.

June 6th

STATELY tree ! Look down on me and teach me how to grow — in grace and strength from year to year. Your secret I would know. Teach me how to stand and face a storm with head unbent — patient and contented with a slow development.

⋄ ⋄ ⋄ ⋄ ⋄ ⋄

June 7th

SEEK the silent places where no jarring sound is heard — and nothing breaks the stillness but the singing of a bird . . . . Nature tells her secrets not to those who hurry by — But to those who walk with quiet heart and seeing eye.

⋄ ⋄ ⋄ ⋄ ⋄ ⋄

June 8th

WE can't expect fine weather and good fortune all the way. The clouds will come, the storms will break and skies will turn to grey. But when you're looking at a cloud that's thick and black and wide — Don't forget the sun is shining on the other side.

June 9th

AS days go by we live and learn and with the years grow wise. We sift the false things from the true and see with clearer eyes. As each birthday comes along we find that we can say— that Time has left a trail of blessings all along the way.

∘ ∘ ∘ ∘ ∘ ∘

June 10th

NEVER think you're wasting time in planning lovely things. Dare to reach out for the rainbow. Let your thoughts take wings. Keep on building all the time your castles in the blue. Keep on dreaming. That's the way to make your dreams come true.

∘ ∘ ∘ ∘ ∘ ∘

June 11th

WHO has had the worst of it and who has had the best ? None can say for each must pass his individual test. Covet nothing, envy none, for all have things to bear. Everything is balanced, God is good and life is fair.

June 12*th*

IF it were always summertime how weary we
should grow — of the fadeless roses and the
sun's unfailing glow.   We'd never stop and listen
if the birds could always sing.   It's twice as sweet
because we know that time is on the wing.

June 13*th*

DISAPPOINTMENTS oftentimes are blessings
in disguise.   The thing you thought you
wanted might have proved a worthless prize.
The shining hopes that came to nothing . . . . Someday you may see — It was all a part of your un-
folding destiny.

June 14*th*

IF you let a patch of ground get overrun with
weeds — You can't expect to raise the blooms
that come from goodly seeds.   It's a law that
runs through life.   You gather as you sow.   So
do not plant a thistle and expect a rose to grow.

June 15th

YOU can smile your way through life or you can fume and fret. It will all depend upon the way your thoughts are set. If they're turned towards the sun you'll always face the light— and you will be guided to horizons broad and bright.

∘ ∘ ∘ ∘ ∘ ∘

June 16th

HERE and there along the road Fate offers you a chance — to change your life and make it something fresh and glorious . . . . A bright new hope comes tapping at the doorways of the heart — bringing Opportunity to make another start.

∘ ∘ ∘ ∘ ∘ ∘

June 17th

SUMMER is the festival of bloom and song and light. The gardens blaze, the air is sweet, the corn is green and bright. It's as if God bids us rub our eyes and look and see — His glory in the loveliness of field and flower and tree.

June 18*th*

MAKE a little time each day for putting wrong things right. For breaking up the gloomy clouds and letting in the light. Make the time for making friends and take some time each day — for counting up the blessings that you've gathered on the way.

June 19*th*

YOU'LL never see the sunshine if you always draw the blind. You'll never make new friendships if you close up heart and mind. You can't expect that happiness is going to come to you. You've got to go and look for it from every point of view.

June 20*th*

CLOSE the Gates of Memory. Come back, my heart, come back. You dare not stray too far along that old forgotten track. There's no returning to the past, so cling not to its sorrow —lest you miss the path that leads unto a bright Tomorrow.

June 21st

WE'D like to bid this moment stay — with meadows green and gardens gay. Roses bloom at sill and door. Midsummer Day is here once more. The beauty of the Spring has fled and Autumn's glory lies ahead. How lovely is this golden time — when the year is at its prime !

June 22nd

THIS my wish for you that you will have the power to see — a gleam of gold through every shadow of adversity. For if you bring a happy heart to each experience — you will always walk the sunlit paths of Providence.

June 23rd

THIS is your day : the day when you can turn a clean new page. You can always start afresh whatever be your age. You're never too old to step out on the road of heart's desire — and change yourself into the kind of person you admire.

June 24th

TRY to find out what you have been sent on earth to do. Find out what your mission is then vow to see it through. Try to find out why you're here and why you've come *this* way. No-one else can fill the part that you were meant to play.

June 25th

LIFE, like Summer, hurries by : a swiftly passing show. But it is useless to regret. It passes. Let it go . . . . Who knows ? Perhaps you'll knock upon Tomorrow's secret door — and find within a happiness you never knew before.

June 26th

STORE the sunshine in the secret places of the heart. Then should shadows fall and all the golden hours depart — you'd still be happy for you'd have the brightness stored away — to bring the memory of June into a winter's day.

June 27th

AGE can hold no threat for you — if you've loved the good and true.   Time's swift pace you'll not lament.   You'll be happy and content— gleaning with a quiet mind—what the years have left behind.

o   o   o   o   o   o

June 28th

THOUGH the pattern of events is hidden from your view.   Rest assured God has a purpose and a plan for you.   Someday in the tapestry you'll see the gold threads shine — discovering the beauty of the ultimate design.

o   o   o   o   o   o

June 29th

HOW God must have loved the world to make such lovely things !   Roses, stars and butter- flies and birds with painted wings.   Rainbows, dawns and sunsets, tree and stream and waterfall. Surely there is Love behind the beauty of it all.

E

June 30th

ON the wings of Memory we rise and fly away—back into the ever-lovely lands of yesterday—We live again the sweetest moments of the by-gone years — disappointments are forgotten—sorrow disappears. Time draws golden veils across the scenes of grief and pain. Birthdays come and birthdays go, but memories remain.

July 1st

GIVE Life time to spin the unseen threads of destiny. Give Life time to solve your problems. Trust and wait and see. Providence has plans for you. Of that there is no doubt. But they can't be hurried. Give Life time to work them out.

July 2nd

IF we cannot see beauty on sunless days when the sky is grey and cold — we'll never see much when the sky is blue and the earth all green and gold . . . . If we cannot see God in the daily round as we hurry here and there — it's doubtful whether we'll ever really find Him anywhere.

July 3rd

EVERY year has its seasons. Every season has its mood. Wild and stormy, gay and happy. Tranquil, quiet and subdued. Every year brings a birthday and it marks another phase —and every season of life is sweet : High Summer . . . . and Autumn days.

July 4th

MAKE your life a house of sunshine, beautiful and gay. A life that shines and gives out light to all who pass your way. Even though you live where there's a grey and gloomy view. You yourself can be a window that the sun comes through.

July 5th

WOULD you really wish to live again those bygone years ? Would you think the joy recaptured would be worth the tears ? We cover the past with rosy veils of glamour and romance. But would you want to live it again if you could have the chance ?

July 6th

GETTING all you've prayed for doesn't always bring content. Learn to take with gratitude what Providence has sent. Often God withholds from us the things for which we pray — and in the end we find that something better comes our way.

∘ ∘ ∘ ∘ ∘ ∘

July 7th

WE'RE only here a little while. We're only passing by. Time has wings and quickly do the golden moments fly. So do not waste a single minute of the precious days. There is something to be gathered out of every phase.

∘ ∘ ∘ ∘ ∘ ∘

July 8th

HOW can you cling to a grief that is old— when God paints the morning all rosy and gold? How can you hold to a sad old regret— when Nature is saying—Rejoice and forget.

∘ ∘ ∘ ∘ ∘ ∘

July 9th

LIFE is full of boons and blessings. Every day they come anew. You will find them if you seek them where you go .... There's a blue patch way out yonder where the clouds are thinning out. Keep on looking and you'll find that it will grow.

July 10*th*

IT doesn't do to plan too carefully,
    To be too sure, too clever or too wise.
Tomorrow's door is locked. God holds the key
Behind it there may be a big surprise.

July 11*th*

ONE who has a birthday on this day,
    From Summer's store can pluck a bright
  bouquet,
Cornflowers, asters, marigolds and stocks,
Lilies and delphiniums and phlox.
Canterbury bells and cherry pie,
All the garnered glory of July.

July 12*th*

THINGS work out if given time so do not
    strive and strain — in a frantic effort to
undo a tangled skein. If your life is fraught with
problems, leave them for today. There **are**
threads you can't unravel in a hurried way.

July 13*th*

EVERY day make someone glad or someone's
faith sustain — and then you'll always know
you have not lived the day in vain . . . . Go out
of your way to warm a heart that's hard and
cold. Give out love and you will find it comes
back sevenfold.

⦾   ⦾   ⦾   ⦾   ⦾   ⦾

July 14*th*

IT was never meant that we should have an easy
task — getting always what we want and
having all we ask . . . . Set-backs check our pro-
gress, slow us down at every turn — but they
give us time to think and that's the way to learn.

⦾   ⦾   ⦾   ⦾   ⦾   ⦾

July 15*th*

DO not fill each passing moment of each busy
day — with the thoughts of worldly matters,
pleasure, work and play. Make a little pause
before the evening shadows fall — to think about
the things that really matter most of all.

July 16*th*

LOOK for beauty and for goodness. Seek them day by day. You will find them on your path wherever you may stray. Don't go looking round for faults and troubles, flaws and woes. We find what we go searching for . . . . for that's the way life goes.

ᴑ   ᴑ   ᴑ   ᴑ   ᴑ   ᴑ

July 17*th*

WORK is not the thing that makes you old and tired and grey. It's the little cares that press about you every day. It's the pin-prick worries that annoy you and depress— robbing you of zest and youth, of health and happiness. Kill them at the very start. Turn them out of mind and heart.

ᴑ   ᴑ   ᴑ   ᴑ   ᴑ   ᴑ

July 18*th*

NEVER shrink from taking a responsibility. Do what is expected of you well and willingly. Do not shirk the extra task but do it with a smile. Bear the added load, if asked, and go the second mile.

July 19*th*

THERE'S one choice that's always right, one road that's always clear — That's the path of duty. Follow this and have no fear. Other signposts may direct to prospects good and gay —Heed them not, but go ahead where duty points the way.

ᴏ   ᴏ   ᴏ   ᴏ   ᴏ   ᴏ

July 20*th*

DO not build a wall around your garden of content.
Life can't be enjoyed alone, and happiness was meant
For all to share, so let your gate stand ever open wide
Someone will be glad to see what's on the other side.

ᴏ   ᴏ   ᴏ   ᴏ   ᴏ   ᴏ

July 21*st*

GIVE me a calm and steadfast will to meet whatever is to be — facing the future unafraid with courage and serenity . . . . Give me tranquillity of mind, a heart content, with all at peace. Lead me, O Lord, down quiet ways. My strength sustain, my faith increase.

July 22nd

SEEK your happiness in things on which you
can depend. Nature offers to her children
pleasures without end : rosy dawns and golden
sunsets, fields and forest bowers. Hills and
mountains, streams and meadows, gardens, birds
and flowers.

July 23rd

WAIT before you wonder what tomorrow may
unfold.
Wait before you worry what the future days may
hold.
Live in hope and confidence. By nothing be
depressed.
Then you'll draw unto yourself the good things
and the best.

July 24th

YOU never know what's waiting at the turning
of the road. Or what the bend is going to
bring in view. When you're least expecting it
a blessing is bestowed. Another vista opens out
for you.

July 25th

IF you put your faith in God you won't be at a loss — when you reach the fateful signpost where the roadways cross. You will feel an unseen hand upon your shoulder laid. The right direction will be seen, the wise decision made.

July 26th

DO not fret and worry over things you cannot change. What's the use of beating at a wall ? Accept the things that have to be — with humour and philosophy. For worrying will do no good at all.

July 27th

CAN this be the garden where a few brief months ago — the bare trees stood with branches bent beneath a weight of snow ? Can this be the little pool that Winter glazed with ice ? Some magic wand has turned it all into a paradise : a fairyland of butterflies, of birds and humming bees. Of fragrant bowers, of gorgeous flowers, green grass and shady trees.

July 28th

LEAN upon the Word of God and it will take your weight. Giving you the strength to face whatever be your fate. It will always hold you up when evil powers assail you. Lean upon the Word of God and it will never fail you.

July 29th

IF we could be given that for which our hearts now ache — would it really prove a blessing, or a big mistake? It's as well we have no choice. It's not for us to say — But to make the best of whatsoever comes our way.

July 30th

LIFE is like a field in which we sow from day to day — seeds of good or evil by the thing we do and say . . . . Some will garner sheaves of joy and some will reap in tears — when they come to gather in the harvest of the years.

July 31*st*

SWIFTLY go the happy days like birds upon the wing. Quickly fly the shining hours when heart and spirit sing. Youth must pass. But why regret when life has passed its prime. Every phase is sweet. It can't be always summertime.

August 1*st*

IF one road is closed to you another you will find. If the way is barred don't give up hope and fall behind. God directs our steps and has a plan for every soul. There are paths you never dreamed of leading to your goal.

August 2*nd*

OFTEN with the years across our eyes a veil is drawn — and we cease to see the vision granted with the dawn . . . . But we never lose it if we wake with gratitude — thanking God each morning for the gift of life renewed.

August 3rd

WHEN a kindred soul we see. We feel that it was meant to be. It seems the work of Providence — and not of blind and fickle chance. For surely it is God who sends — the happiness we find in friends.

o o o o o o

August 4th

IT would be a dreary world, a place of gloom and greed — were it not for those who try to live the Christian's creed . . . . These things keep us linked with God wherever we may be — and glorify this bad old world : Faith, Hope and Charity.

o o o o o o

August 5th

MANY yearn for better things but shrink from sudden change — because they lack the courage for adventures new and strange . . . . Grasp your opportunities in faith and not in fear. Nothing worth the having can be won without a tear.

August 6th

S HOW the spirit of good-will in all you do and say. Let your life your inner faith express . . . . Put your heart into your task, your creed into your day — and let your work proclaim what you profess.

August 7th

W HEN things turn against you and there's nothing left but dreams. When unlucky circumstances cut across your schemes. Turn it to advantage. Snatch a pearl out of the dust. Make misfortune teach you how to wait and hope and trust.

August 8th

T HERE'S no need to wander far for oppor- tunity. Look around just where you are and you will surely see — Somebody in need of someone. Might it not be you ? Somebody in need of something . . . . something you can do.

August 9th

WHETHER life be calm and fair or winds of sorrow blow — Trust . . . . though every hope be lost to view. In the deeps and in the shallows be content to go — where the winds of God are driving you.

August 10th

IT is foolish to lament the passing of the years. Useless to regret the wasted hours with sighs and tears. Round and round the clock will go whatever you may say. So take with grateful heart what Life bestows on you today. The present hour is yours to live. Enjoy all that it has to give.

August 11th

IT'S the little things of life that prove just what we are. What we say can charm and please or it can hurt and jar. It's the little things that test — and show us at our worst or best.

August 12th

FROWN into your mirror and you'll see what others see — when you are disgruntled or depressed . . . . Don't help Time to draw the wrinkles. Live life cheerfully — and show the world your bright side and your best.

August 13th

THE things that you anticipate and plan for eagerly — will often disappoint you bitterly. While the unexpected thing the greatest thrill of all will bring — and leave behind the sweetest memory.

August 14th

HUMAN hearts need sympathy and that is why God sends — consolations through the understanding of our friends . . . . Trouble would be twice as hard with nobody to share it — no good companion at your side to help you grin and bear it.

August 15th

TURN your thoughts to other people when your life looks blank and drear. There is always someone needing strength and comfort, hope and cheer . . . . Help yourself by helping others ill in body or in mind. Easing someone else's pain your own salvation you will find.

o   o   o   o   o   o

August 16th

OUT into the unknown future be prepared to move — even though it means you have to leave your cosy groove. Fresh conditions may confront you. Face them hopefully. Changes often force the door of opportunity.

o   o   o   o   o   o

August 17th

THERE'S always a solution when a problem you've been set. There always is a way in which the challenge can be met. There always is a means of getting over every fence — with just a little patience and a bit of common sense.

F

August 18*th*

TAKING all things into account life's really not so bad — though there are so many people who are sour and sad . . . . The picture has another side. Much happiness you'll find — if you look with seeing eyes and seek with open mind.

August 19*th*

IF you can't smile a lot smile a little. Though it's only a few times a day. If the smiles never come — you'll get solemn and glum — and your face will start growing that way.

August 20*th*

TROUBLES come ; that is true. But the blessings come too. And whatever God sends we must take it . . . . There are hills to ascend, but you find in the end — That life is as good as you make it.

August 21*st*

FACE the problems of today. That's all you need to do. Deal with them according to the strength that's given you. Don't anticipate the hour until you hear it chime. We were meant to live this life just one day at a time.

August 22*nd*

UP and down the countryside the golden sheaves now stand. And a rich fulfilment crowns the labours of the land. Satisfying to the heart and pleasing to the eye : the pattern of the harvest fields beneath the August sky.

August 23*rd*

WE all arrive by different roads at the appointed place. Each one has his star to follow and his path to trace. It's not the pace that matters as we go upon our way. It's what we really are when we get home at close of day.

August 24th

NO secret key will open the Gates of Yesterday — when once they've closed behind us.
We have to make our way — along the path that
opens upon the present scene — Not gazing back
in longing on things that might have been.

o o o o o o

August 25th

HEAVEN would be out of reach
And God would be a God afar,
If Faith had never set a ladder
Up against the highest star.

o o o o o o

August 26th

I RECALL the happiness — no heartaches and
no tears. Only what was best and sweetest
of the golden years. I remember all the rapture
and forget the pain. It is always Summer when
I walk in Memory Lane.

August 27th

THE Inn of Friendship lights the way along life's winding path. The door stands ever open and a fire burns on the hearth. The lamp gives forth a glow of welcome and a kindly ray. Comforting the hearts of all who travel by that way.

o   o   o   o   o   o

August 28th

THANK you for your friendship. It has meant so much to me. Thank you for your understanding, love and sympathy. You have helped and guided me through many an anxious day. How different life would be if you had never come my way.

o   o   o   o   o   o

August 29th

TIME from our eyes wipes the tears away. A miracle happens. We wake one day — to discover that life has much to give. We find new hope and the will to live. From out of the shadows sweet voices call. The voices that tell us that Time heals all.

August 30th

S UNLIGHT breaking through the mist. The birches turning gold. Crimson dahlias tall and lovely. Sunflowers bright and bold. Fruited branches in the orchards with their burdens bend. Peace and plenty crown the golden days at Summer's end.

August 31st

W E do not climb high mountains by gazing in a dream — At the heights above us where the bright crags gleam. Great tasks are not accomplished within a single day. We have to work with patience and struggle all the way.

September 1st

N OW the orchard boughs are hung with apples ripe and bright — russet, red and yellow in the mellow golden light . . . . Once again the ladder stands against the laden spray — a touch of Autumn in the air : the first September day.

September 2nd

IT'S the root that is the strength of any plant
or flower or tree : the root that feeds the
fruiting bough, the secret part that none can see
. . . . We, too, must have roots in life, and when
the storms blow wild and cold — we shall not
break, but stand up straight . . . . because the
hidden roots will hold.

September 3rd

" BEAR ye one another's burdens "
Seeing the unspoken need,
Do your part to ease the strain
By kindly word and gracious deed.

September 4th

ISN'T it a blessing that you can't spend all day
long — thinking of the many things that keep
on going wrong . . . . Always there are jobs that
must be done without delay. If it weren't for
work we'd very soon grow old and grey.

September 5th

SOULS, like babes, are weak and small. Unless God holds us up we fall. How can we find the strength to stand — if we do not take His hand ?

o   o   o   o   o   o

September 6th

LEARN to take things easily. Don't fuss and fume and fret. When your will is thwarted and your plans are all upset — Don't push at a bolted door and dry to force a way. Just accept the situation. Live from day to day.

o   o   o   o   o   o

September 7th

LIFE'S a jig-saw puzzle and when first you look at it — You wonder how you're ever going to make the pieces fit . . . . But take your time and bit by bit the picture you will see — as the fragments come together, fitting perfectly.

September 8th

OLD friends may be dear, but let us never turn away — from the chance to make new friends — for there may be a day — when changes come as come they must. Time passes. Ways divide. Grateful we may be to find a new friend at our side. So never say that it's too late another heart to win. Another door to open, a new friendship to begin.

o   o   o   o   o   o

September 9th

THIS is my birthday. A new year beginning, I'm tired of the goals that are not worth the winning.
I want a new hope, a new song, a new part
I want a new road, a new life, a new heart.
And this is the moment to drop the old theme,
To make a fresh start and to dream a new dream.

o   o   o   o   o   o

September 10th

IF along the path of life we've sown the hidden seeds — Of friendship, love and sympathy, good thoughts and kindly deeds . . . . Always there'll be flowers to pick, a fresh bloom every day — from the seeds we've sown between the stones along the way.

September 11th

IF endless happiness is your aim
   A joy that will burn with a lasting flame,
It's a garden you're needing, a patch of ground
To love and to work for the whole year round.

September 12th

YOU'VE got to put your back into the work
   you want to do — and put up with the part
of it that is a bore for you. You've got to do
the drudgery and make the sacrifice. For success
in anything you've got to pay the price.

September 13th

IF smiling lips and shining eyes in the looking
   glass you see. You need not fear the passing
years for young you'll always be. Joy imparts a
beauty Time can't touch, and that's a truth.
Happiness is better than the passing bloom of
youth.

September 14th

SEASON of fruitfulness ! Golden September
   Summer's bright splendour we swiftly forget,
Autumn brings plenty and peace and fulfilment.
There is no time to repine or regret.

September 15th

TIME grant to you the harvesting of dreams. And the success of all your dearest schemes. And after harvest when the fields seem bare — O may you glean and find a blessing there.

September 16th

I WOULD hold this Autumn beauty. Bid the lovely season stay. I would halt the striding year and keep it at this golden day. But the glory must depart ; the leaves must fade and fall to earth — that Nature may commence her work of resurrection and rebirth.

September 17th

FORGET the times of trouble, but not the truths they taught. Forget the days of sorrow, but not the strength they brought. Forget the storms you battled through beneath a heavy load — but not the light that led you safely down the unknown road.

September 18th

WE worship not a God remote but One who loves us here and now. A King with wounds upon His hands and crown of thorns upon His brow . . . . The Friend of man ! He stands and watches at the gateways of the heart— Waiting to be called upon when other comforters depart.

September 19th

HOPE needs no staff to lean upon,
     No helping hand, no guiding star,
Over horizons lost to view, outstripping dreams
Hope travels far.

September 20th

MAY your good ship soon come home upon the evening tide
Sailing into harbour with her canvas spreading wide.
Laden with the things for which you've sighed and worked and prayed,
The cargo that you thought was lost ; the blessing long delayed.

September 21st

FROM the eyes of God I cannot hide. I feel His Presence ever at my side. What is this Love that holds and haunts me so ? What is this thing that will not let me go ?

September 22nd

LOOKING out into the future down the pathway of the years. You won't see the bright horizon if your eyes are blurred with tears. You will miss the wayside flowers around your present pathway set — if you cling to memories that fill your heart with vain regret.

September 23rd

JUST a few brief weeks ago the fields were gold with ripened grain. Now across the bare brown stubbles ploughs are moving once again— Making furrows for new sowings, getting ready for the Spring. So that in the days to come there'll be another harvesting.

September 24th

IN the gardens leaves are turning. Bright leaves whirl about the square. Along the windy street they dance. A festal touch is in the air . . . . Up the walls and round the sills in city street and country lane — Autumn hangs her glowing garlands as the creepers fade again.

September 25th

A GATE that opens in the shadows often proves for you — to be a place of blessedness where life begins anew . . . . The very thing that causes trouble, heartache and distress — often brings much benefit and ends in happiness.

September 26th

DOORS may close, but windows open, letting in the sun. God never leaves us in the dark, but gives to everyone — the power to look with eyes of hope towards a brighter view. Though He bolts and bars the door, He opens windows too.

September 27th

IF the heart is young — you'll always keep your dreams. Through the darkest cloud you'll catch the golden gleams. If with every dawn your hopes and prayers ascend. Life will be for you a Summer without end.

September 28th

I PRAY that I may always hold to all the faith that I profess. That I may do my Master's bidding, serving Him in steadfastness. That Life might be a pilgrimage towards the highest and the best ; a sacrament, a bold adventure and a great and glorious quest.

September 29th

KEEP on singing though there's none to hear. Keep on smiling though there's none to cheer.
Keep on ploughing though you've reaped no crops.
Keep on marching if the drummer stops.

September 30th

THERE will be higher hills to climb and stronger foes to conquer yet. There will be greater loads to bear and more temptations to be met. Do not suppose the road gets smoother as the winding way you wend. You will need God's help and guidance right on to the journey's end.

o o o o o o

October 1st

NONE need go without refreshment in the heat of day.
It is there for all who thirst upon the dusty way.
Comfort for the weary heart and joy for all who weep,
Pardon for the penitent. The wells of God are deep.

o o o o o o

October 2nd

JEWELS of wisdom are locked in The Book. The riches are hidden. But if we will look With patience and faith and a diligent mind The treasure is there for the seeker to find.

October 3rd

MEMORY casts a golden ray in every secret place. We see old scenes out of the past, a loved and smiling face. The friendship long remembered and the name forever dear. We recall when birthdays come to mark another year.

o   o   o   o   o   o

October 4th

THE ear of Faith can hear the music coming from afar — even when there's discord, words that hurt and sounds that jar . . . . The eye of faith can range beyond the place where shadows fall — seeing sunshine in the dark . . . . and God's love over all.

o   o   o   o   o   o

October 5th

"BETTER country farther on." So said the pioneers — who beat a trail into the wilds and tamed with toil and tears — the hostile land. They fought with Nature, challenging her hold— wresting slowly from her grasp, the grass, the grain, the gold. In their hearts a great faith shone — in better country farther on.

G

October 6th

BURN what summer leaves behind in the autumn hours. Broken stalks, decaying weeds, dead wood and faded flowers. Burn the rubbish of the past. Pile it on the pyre. Grievances and grudges . . . . Fling them all upon the fire.

October 7th

GIVE me the happy things of life.
    A heart that's merry all the way.
An outlook that is broad and bright,
A spirit that is brave and gay.

October 8th

THE kind of person you will be depends in every way — on the sort of person you are being now, today. Have a warm and kindly heart and when your hands you fold — You'll be happy — You'll be wanted . . . . Loved when you are old.

October 9th

DO the thing you have to do and do it faithfully.   Consecrate the commonplace wherever you may be.   Someone may be influenced
by what you say and do.   Somebody may learn
a lesson just by watching you.

October 10th

EVERY day's a new adventure, never lived
before.   Fresh experience awaits you.   New
things lie in store.   You can ask to be set free
from every binding chain.   You can be forgiven
and can start your life again.

October 11th

THE choice is yours to fall or rise, to injure
or to bless.   To fill a room with gloom or
light it up with happiness.   To use or waste the
precious hours, to work or take your ease.   To
walk the path of duty or to go the way you please.

October 12th

TIME unfolds our destiny
    As the years go by we'll see
If our way was wrong or right.
Time will bring the truth to light.

○ ○ ○ ○ ○ ○

October 13th

THERE are times when it's hard to keep fighting.
    There are times when you'd like to give in,
But the one who holds on when the last hope has
    gone
Is the one who is certain to win.

○ ○ ○ ○ ○ ○

October 14th

HAPPINESS is catching ! smile and give it
    out.   Other folks will take it once it gets
about.   Laughter is infectious ! Gloomy moods
suppress.   Start an epidemic, spreading happiness.

○ ○ ○ ○ ○ ○

October 15th

THERE'S something to be gained from every
    loss we have to bear — something to be
garnered from the harvests of despair.   There's
something to be prized in every friendship that
we make.   There is something we can give and
something we can take.

October 16th

WHAT if you're not quite so young as you were — and there is grey in the gold? Time's passing swiftly for everyone else. Why should you mind growing old? We should be able to say in our hearts, nearing the end of the way. " Thank You, dear God, for a wonderful time. It's been a beautiful day."

October 17th

DO not cross your bridges before they come in view.
Wait until you're there before deciding what to do.
Wait before anticipating trouble, tears and loss.
The bridge you dread may prove to be an easy one to cross.

October 18th

THE Master came on earth to save the Gentile and the Jew. He came to lift our vision to a wider, grander view. He came to turn the thoughts of men away from self and sin — and to tell the tidings that God's kingdom is within.

October 19*th*

DO not cling too closely to the human reckon-
ings,
Time is nothing when we think of the eternal
things.
Do not count the years as you are looking back
today
But the blessings they have brought you all along
the way.

⌀ ⌀ ⌀ ⌀ ⌀ ⌀

October 20*th*

QUIET are the woods for the song birds are
dumb
Knowing the hint of the winter is come,
Hushed is the garden and silent the lane,
But there'll be sunshine and music again.
This is the promise to which we shall cling
While we are waiting and dreaming of Spring.

⌀ ⌀ ⌀ ⌀ ⌀ ⌀

October 21*st*

NEVER drop out of the race before the course
is run. Don't admit of failure or defeat to
anyone. And if a thing looks difficult — Don't
say it can't be done . . . . before you've tried.

October 22nd

IN God's love we find an answer to the restless thought : and we find the peace for which our weary minds have sought. In the silence we are quietened by a touch divine. When we bow our heads and say, Not my will, Lord, but Thine.

October 23rd

TIME proves the worth of friends, tests them and tries them. Life alters many things, changing our view. Tearing the mask from the false and the trivial. Making us value the real and the true.

October 24th

YOU can't afford to stoop or falter underneath the strain — of long remembered grievances and unforgotten pain . . . . God offers you the future. You refuse or you accept. You can make your choice. It's yours to take or to reject.

October 25th

THE sun is fickle and uncertain going in and out. But we can make a little bit of sun to spread about — by friendliness and cheery words, bright looks and merry ways — to hearten and to help each other through the sunless days.

○　○　○　○　○　○

October 26th

WHEN we see the changing seasons pass before the eye. We feel there are unfailing laws on which we can rely. We sense a Mind behind it all when Nature's work we scan — We feel there is a meaning and a purpose and a plan.

○　○　○　○　○　○

October 27th

EVERY passing phase of life brings something to remember. April dreams, the joys of June, the harvests of September. Autumn with its mellow beauty has its compensations. Winter, too, brings to the heart its own quiet consolations.

October 28th

MANY chance acquaintances are met from day to day. Many fall in step with us along life's winding way — But few there are to whom we give the sacred name of friend. They who with unfailing love keep faith unto the end.

October 29th

IT is love and love alone that makes life bearable. Lifts it from the commonplace and makes it beautiful. Gives to it a meaning and a motive high and fine — touching it with something that is more than half divine.

October 30th

FROM my window I can see
　　The stark bare branches of a tree.
It seems no sap could ever flow
Through those boughs. And yet I know
That when I see the April rain
The tree will come to life again.

October 31st

THE Spring has its glory of daffodil gold,
　　When primroses open and green buds
　　unfold.
But sometimes I think as I watch the leaves fall
That Autumn's fair days are the fairest of all.

November 1st

WELCOME what each season brings, the
　　sunshine or the snow. The Summertime
was sweet, but it has gone, so let it go . . . . Happy
is the heart that sings when skies are dark and
grey — hearing on November winds the nightin-
gales of May.

November 2nd

IN everything give thanks to God. Look round
　　you and behold — unremembered benefits and
blessings manifold . . . . Strokes of fortune, lucky
chances, mercies of past days. You will find
you have been led and blessed in many ways.

November 3rd

THERE'S always the garden to keep you young when days turn bleak and cold. Folks who love a garden are a long time growing old. Never do their minds grow weary weaving lovely schemes. Planning in the winter hours the garden of their dreams.

* * * * * *

November 4th

"LEAVE it till tomorrow" says the tempter cunningly — knowing when tomorrow comes that there will surely be — something to divert us from the course we would pursue. An excuse for putting off the good we meant to do.

* * * * * *

November 5th

NO-ONE wants to weep with you if you are always sad. Lonely you will never be if you are brave and glad. Search the clouds. You're bound to spot a gleam of light to follow. Though today looks grim and grey. Remember there's tomorrow !

November 6th

THERE comes a time when courage falters and your spirits fail — When happiness seems far away and faith of no avail . . . . When hopes trail in the dust like faded banners once so bright. That is just the moment when you have to stand and fight.

⊙   ⊙   ⊙   ⊙   ⊙   ⊙

November 7th

NATURE does not rush from summer blue to winter grey.
We are given time to watch the glory fade away.
Time to see the changing colours of the countryside
As we stroll along the golden lanes of Autumntide.

⊙   ⊙   ⊙   ⊙   ⊙   ⊙

November 8th

FORTUNE brings to happy harbours all whose sails are rightly set — if a strong hand's on the wheel and every gale is bravely met . . . . Dream your dream. You'll be rewarded when you watch with joy and pride — the argosies you launched returning — homeward on the evening tide.

November 9th

WITS' End Corner is the place where many roadways meet. For some it means catastrophe, disaster and defeat . . . . For others it's the place where first they learn to kneel and pray. Here God puts a fingerpost to show lost souls the way.

o o o o o o

November 10th

THEY who lay aside their weapons on the battlefield — instead of struggling on with broken sword and shattered shield — do not know the glow of pride that crowns a fight well won : a goal achieved, a task completed and a duty done.

o o o o o o

November 11th

DOWN the lanes and in the woodlands leafy carpets have been spread : rust and russet, bronze and amber, gold and copper, brown and red. Stripped of all their autumn glory, trees stand stricken and austere — just as if they stood in silence for the dying of the year.

November 12th

WHEN Youth has had its shining hour and Love its golden day. Time may fade the colours and the glory pass away — But something of the magic lingers, never to depart — deep down in the secret places of a quiet heart.

November 13th

DON'T assume you've lots of time for all you mean to do. Though the future seems to stretch away into the blue . . . . Maybe you intend to scale those summits far away — but all that matters is the hill you've got to climb today.

November 14th

OTHER people's problems . . . . What are they to you ? Maybe you could solve them if you wanted to. Do not shrug your shoulders and turn the other way. Other people's troubles might be yours one day.

November 15th

NEVER doubt God has a purpose. Someday you will see — the pattern He is working on the looms of destiny. Much is hidden. All the colours cannot show and shine — But every thread is needed to complete the great design.

❧ ❧ ❧ ❧ ❧ ❧

November 16th

WE cannot find Life's treasure if we're rushing here and there — chasing shadows through the crowds and beating at the air . . . . Draw apart. Be still and pray when weary and hard-pressed. " Come unto Me " the Master said, " and I will give you rest."

❧ ❧ ❧ ❧ ❧ ❧

November 17th

ON the hills and in the valleys
    Sorrows fade and hopes ascend,
All roads lead to bright horizons
In the company of friends.

November 18*th*

YOU were not put into this world mere pleasure to pursue — or to gain material success . . . . But to find the work that God intended you to do. This alone brings lasting happiness.

November 19*th*

THERE is a philosophy in flower and forest, field and fen — higher than the lofty thoughts upon the lips of learned men . . . . There's a gospel of salvation in the song of every bird — for those whose hearts can understand the hidden truth, the secret word.

November 20*th*

BELIEVE in your God and lean on Him in failure and success. This is the secret of a life of hope and happiness. This is what brings a magic meaning to all happenings. This is the truth that glorifies dull days **and** common things.

November 21st

USE your gifts. Don't let them rest or they will rust away. Take the opportunities that come with every day. By perseverance, self-reliance and self-discipline — You can be what you desire. The kingdom is within.

ᴏ ᴏ ᴏ ᴏ ᴏ ᴏ

November 22nd

NO good deed is ever wasted and no kind word said in vain. The good we do to other people Life returns to us again. No good deed is lost to God although it may be lost to view. Cast your bread upon the waters. Time will bring it back to you.

ᴏ ᴏ ᴏ ᴏ ᴏ ᴏ

November 23rd

NOWHERE'S too far for a dream to go.
    For a dream can outrun the winds that
        blow
And take a rainbow in its stride,
Waiting not for time or tide.

H

November 24th

LIFE without love is a meaningless story.
    Love is the answer, the power and the glory.
Love is the lamp on the untrodden road,
Lighting the way to the heart's true abode.

      o   *o*   *o*   *o*   *o*   *o*

November 25th

THE last leaves lie upon the grass. Why, oh why must Beauty ? Why must all the glory go ? Such is the law ; it must be so. The leaves must fall at Winter's breath — and trees stand stricken, feigning death . . . . And yet I hear the robin sing. He knows there'll be another Spring.

      o   *o*   *o*   *o*   *o*   *o*

November 26th

STOP and lend a friendly hand
    To heal the hurt and ease the strain,
Be the good Samaritan.
You will not pass this way again.

November 27th

DO not try to drift along through life without a creed. Cultivate your own philosophy .... Something that will give you in the moment of your need : wisdom, courage and serenity.

November 28th

IT is folly to be out upon life's crowded road— if you do not know the meaning of the highway code .... Read the rules. They're in the Bible, there for you to learn. You will need to follow them at every twist and turn.

November 29th

THE turning points of life aren't always noticed at the time. Close against the ear the hour of destiny may chime — and we unheeding may not be aware that it has struck. Afterwards we see the point at which we changed our luck.

November 30th

OFTEN in this life we don't appear to travel far. We want to get ahead and hitch our wagon to a star — but it's God who sets the pace. In time we realise — the hindrance we resented was a blessing in disguise.

December 1st

FAR away the Winter seemed, a thought I could not entertain — when the roses threaded garlands through the hedges in the lane . . . . But now it's come I'm well content, for knowing that it must be so — I seek again the quiet joys of home and hearth and firelight glow.

December 2nd

ROUND the gates of Winter when the fogs come thick and grey — the lovely late chrysanthemums their gorgeous blooms display. Nature, ever provident, has paused to scatter here — flowers for the burial of the departing year.

December 3rd

HAPPY thoughts can change our lives. They're stronger than we guess. Happy thoughts uplift the heart with power to heal and bless . . . . Happy thoughts are magic forces working secretly — to establish in our lives health peace and harmony.

December 4th

BENEATH the bleak and bitter skies — Grey and still the garden lies — But out there in the damp and cold — There is a spray of fairy gold — a touch of beauty in the gloom. The Winter jasmine is in bloom.

December 5th

SOMEDAY you'll recall how nothing went the way you planned — and everything seemed cloaked in hopelessness . . . . But looking back you'll find it was a Providential hand that guided you to ultimate success.

December 6th

THIS is a world where people do and say the strangest things. So do not be surprised at bark or bite. This is a world that's all mixed up, a world of smiles and stings — So try to see it in a kindly light.

December 7th

IF you scan the sky and cannot see a golden glow — Make some sunshine for yourself and take it where you go. When there's none up there amongst the clouds as grey as stone. Try to make a little bit of sunshine of your own.

December 8th

EVERY time temptations you defy
    By being firm and keeping standards high,
When good is done, peace kept and kind words said,
The devil loses . . . . And you win instead.

December 9th

IT doesn't cost much to do the kindly and the gracious thing — To strike the note that puts an end to strife and quarrelling . . . . It doesn't take long to do those little acts of courtesy — that lift the tone of life and make it run harmoniously.

December 10th

THE habit of hurry, the habit of worry when things are not going your way. That is what makes life dim and dull instead of rich and gay . . . . The habit of moping when you should be hoping — no matter how hard be your case. These are the habits that draw the telltale wrinkles on the face.

December 11th

LITTLE mustard seeds of faith can work great miracles — Moving mountains that you thought were mighty obstacles — Breaking down old barriers and making all things new . . . . Little mustard seeds of prayer can change the world for you.

December 12th

EACH to his path. By many ways God guides all pilgrim feet. And somewhere in His kingdom There's a place where all roads meet.

December 13th

DO you look for snags or for the good in everything ? Do you give your thoughts an upward or a downward swing ? Life is what you make it by your mental attitude — and blessings come to those who face it in a hopeful mood.

December 14th

WE'RE all outward bound on a voyage to a country far away. To a haven beyond the horizons where the darkness meets the day. But whether we drift in the doldrums or must fight with the gale's full force — We all need to pray for the Pilot to keep us on our course.

December 15th

YOU cannot walk the same road twice. Your steps you can't retrace. By tomorrow you'll be heading for some other place . . . . So carry out that good intention now without delay. You won't pass by this way again ; so take your chance today.

December 16th

GOD gives us memories for our Decembers
        Something to comfort when darkness
        descends,
Things to recall as we dream by the embers,
Heart-warming thoughts of old times and old
    friends.

              o   o   o   o   o   o

December 17th

THE days grow short . . . . The garden now is
stripped of leaves and flowers — but there
are other joys to cheer the heart and speed the
hours . . . . Though Winter be unwelcome it is
Wintertime that brings : the peace of Christmas
and the dear delight of homely things.

              o   o   o   o   o   o

December 18th

TIME moves on and changes come, for no one
can stand still. Yet it is upon our past we
build for good or ill. All whose paths have
crossed our own upon life's winding way — have
helped to shape us and to make us what we are
today.

December 19*th*

THIS is the time to think of giving. Nigh two thousand years ago — To the world God gave His Son. What greater gift could Love bestow ? We, then, with a willing hand should share the good that we possess — passing on our boons and blessings, giving help and happiness.

o   o   o   o   o   o

December 20*th*

THE merry days, the happy days, the days of long ago — come back in remembrance when we watch the red logs glow. The April days, the autumn days, the gold days and the drear ; mingle in the dreams that haunt this season of the years.

o   o   o   o   o   o

December 21*st*

IF you have been wandering down many dark and doubtful ways. Let the Babe of Bethlehem now lead you back to childhood days . . . . If life's treasure you would find — the peace that lasts for evermore — Go you with a childlike heart and knock upon the stable door.

December 22nd

IN the wide warm chimney-corner there's an inglenook of dreams ; a secret place, a quiet place, where shadows play and firelight gleams— and if the dreamer speaks no word, but waits and listens silently — Someone to his hearth will hasten : one whose name is Memory.

December 23rd

JUST as April brings new life to every sleeping tree. Joy is quickened at the time of the Nativity. Life and faith are now renewed by thoughts of holy things. Christmas brings to every door the sound of angel wings. Though wintry storms around us roll. It is the Spring-time of the soul.

December 24th

CHRISTMASTIME is like a lamp that lights the closing year. A lamp that radiates a glow of charity and cheer. A lamp that burns at every window with a golden ray — and warms the heart in winter when the world seems cold and grey.

December 25th

ONCE again it is the birthday of the King of
    Kings
Once again we meditate on high and holy things.
Once again we hear great tidings ringing round
    the earth
The wondrous and amazing story of a Saviour's
    birth.

❧   ❧   ❧   ❧   ❧   ❧

December 26th

WE never reach horizons for they fade into
    the blue. They recede as we advance
towards the distant view. That's the way it is
in Life. There's always something more. Some
new dream to spur us on and fresh fields to
explore.

❧   ❧   ❧   ❧   ❧   ❧

December 27th

LET the Old Year pass away. Mourn not, but
    greet the New. Turn your eyes in faith
towards the peaks that beckon you. Know that
you'll be guided safely down the unmapped road
—given light to see your way and strength to
bear your load.

December 28th

IF we build high walls around the gardens of our lives — no root of love puts forth a bloom, no seed of virtue thrives . . . . God is Light and light we need to make Life's colours glow. Without the sunshine in our hearts how can the flowers grow ?

❧ ❧ ❧ ❧ ❧ ❧

December 29th

AS December dies away you turn your thoughts again — to all that it has brought to you of pleasure and of pain. And as you cast a backward glance on all that lies behind — Do you not feel thankful as the blessings come to mind ?

❧ ❧ ❧ ❧ ❧ ❧

December 30th

LIFE offers compensations for our troubles and our care. Consolations shed their light around us everywhere. Things that make life worth the living : blessings great and small. The things through which God speaks to us . . . . Take comfort from them all.

December 31*st*

THE garden sleeps, the woods are bare. No song breaks through the trees. No golden note comes rippling on the cold and bitter breeze. But the music is to come ! We know it to be true. There'll be thrushes on the bough and sky-larks in the blue.

D1627287